OUTDOOR ROOMS

ROCKPORT PUBLISHERS

DESIGNS FOR PORCHES, TERRACES, DECKS, GAZEBOS

Julie D. Taylor
Foreword by Barbara Barry

First published in the United States of America by:
Rockport Publishers, Inc.
33 Commercial Street
Gloucester, Massachusetts 01930-5089
Telephone: (978) 282-9590
Facsimile: (978) 283-2742
www.rockpub.com

ISBN 1-56496-765-4

10

Book Designer:
The Design Company

Cover Image Designers:
Front Cover: Gian Franco Brignone
Back Cover (top): Roy McMakin
(bottom): Diego Villaseñor

Pages 2–3: Alexander Gorlin

Printed in China

This book is dedicated to the memory of Barry Lee.

ACKNOWLEDGMENTS

My thanks and respect to all the designers, architects, landscapers, homeowners, and photographers who lent their talents to this book. A heartfelt appreciation to Barbara Barry, who is so generous with her poetic words and spirit. To Rosalie Grattaroti at Rockport Publishers: thanks for asking. I also want to acknowledge the support of my clients, my family, and wonderful friends throughout this process, and to my assistant, Linda Won, for keeping me and the office organized and running. And, finally, thanks, always, to Mark McIntire, who continues to teach me so much.

JULIE D. TAYLOR

The publisher would like to thank John Aves for his support of the project.

▲ Landscape Architecture: Rob Steiner
Photograph: Steven A. Gunther

CONTENTS

◀ Design: Charlie Hess and Mayita Dinos
Photograph: Tim Street-Porter

FOREWORD

Architecture: Arthur Erickson
Design: Barbara Barry
Photograph: Tim Street-Porter

I remember the first time I got to sleep outdoors. It was with my sisters in the backyard in our own concoction of a tented room—sheets attached to broomsticks, and what have you. The sense of mystery and magic of doing normal activities in an outdoor space began right there.

My first trip to Italy dining al fresco on the terrace of the Splendido Hotel overlooking the Adriatic under an ancient vine-covered pergola left me changed. It personified the elegance and sensuality of what an outdoor room should be.

Living in Los Angeles affords one the luxury of sleeping with the windows open year-round, and on those special nights when the full moon is up, I open the French doors and let the magic light and the smell of roses and jasmine spill in.

On nights like these I return to that childhood experience, remembering that we are creatures that respond to nature. We are nature at our very best, and anytime and anyway we can return to it, it restores us.

Is it any wonder after all we have created, that we are heading back towards simplicity and nature? We are drawn, I believe, almost magnetically to these outdoor spaces—places where we are able to embrace our essential selves.

BARBARA BARRY
LOS ANGELES

▼ Design: Barbara Barry
Photograph: Tim Street-Porter

INTRODUCTION

Architecture came about from our need to be sheltered from the environment. Throughout history, however, domestic architecture has provided that shelter in ways that have brought us increasingly closer to the elements. Inherent in the human psyche is the desire to "have it all"—to live indoors, protected, and yet continue to experience the outdoors. Creative souls, such as architects and designers, have continually found ways for people to enjoy both.

The choice to explore outdoor living is synonymous with freedom and joy. In 1929, eschewing European Classicism and oppression, architect Rudolph Schindler embraced his new-found home of Los Angeles by creating outdoor sleeping porches in a landmark home that continues to inspire young architects today.

This book will explore bringing the outdoors in and the indoors out. Building on the legendary work of Schindler, and other early twentieth-century architects and designers who redefined the boundaries between indoors and outdoors, we'll look at how home design in the 1990s accommodates and celebrates outdoor living.

The importance and value of connection with the outdoors has increased in the early 1990s, for a variety of reasons: redefinition of leisure time, concerns for the natural environment, and the known healing powers of light and nature. In these pages, we'll see numerous examples of how designers, architects, and homeowners have fashioned their outdoor spaces for maximum comfort, ease, and aesthetics.

▲ Architecture: Josh Schweitzer
Photograph: Tom Bonner

▼ Architecture: John Staff, AIA
Photograph: J. Scott Smith

Some rooms are connected to the outdoors by materials, such as adobe walls. For others, a layer of transparency—glass or screen—define the space. But, who says a room has to have four walls? What defines a room in our context is analogous to the distinction between house and home. Intimacy and intent are the criteria.

As we are taking the definition of room and stretching it, so will we interpret the word *outdoor*. We will first look at spaces that are interior by strict definition but whose purpose is to include, ring in, and possess the outdoors: screened-in porches, rooms of glass with light, air, and nature streaming in. These spaces bring the "outside in."

Keeping with the main structure of the house, we'll then look to spaces that are "hanging on"—porches, entries, terraces, decks, and rooftops. These flat planes are blank slates for creative use of space. "Breaking free" from the house describes spaces that through structure, furnishings, and plantings combine to create the atmosphere and ambiance of a room in open, flat space, such as a courtyard, garden, or pool area.

One-room spaces that bring the "inside out" may be fully enclosed pool houses or greenhouses, or partially open pavilions and gazebos. These buildings are often given greater freedom and folly in their design, as they are usually leisure structures or personal retreats.

And finally, when it comes to "filling up" any of these outdoor rooms, we'll show a great variety of furniture, lighting, and accessories designed for enjoying and preserving outdoor living.

▲ Architecture: Alexander Gorlin
Photograph: Michael Moran

▼ Design: Annie Kelly
Photograph: Tim Street-Porter

OUTSIDE IN

From the *trompe l'oeil* wall paintings of far-away vistas found in ancient Pompeii to Philip Johnson's Glass House, where hardly a mullion blocks the view of his Connecticut estate, people have hungered for a feeling of the outdoors in their protected, interior living spaces. As homeowners become more involved in their garden spaces and live outdoors more, they also want their indoor spaces to be veritable windows on their world.

Traditionally, these indoor/outdoor spaces are breakfast rooms and porch sitting areas. We'll see, however, that the rest of the house can enjoy these spaces in the form of all-glass areas, with light and nature invited into living rooms, bedrooms, and bathrooms.

◄ ► These two sunrooms form just part of the indoor/outdoor areas of a house in the exclusive and beautiful area of Broad Beach in southern California. Angular bay windows allow ocean views and let the light in, setting the stage for the plush and comfort of deep-pile upholstery and leather furniture in the interiors. Angular bay windows are used again in the upper-level master bedroom. Both sunrooms afford visual access to the terraces beyond.

Architecture: David Lawrence Gray, FAIA
Design: Schlesinger & Associates
Photographs: Tim Street-Porter

GLASS HOUSES

There are many advantages to living in an all-glass room (never mind that maxim about not throwing stones!). Light and views are allowed in, while harsh elements are kept out. Vast expanses of glass have connoted closeness to nature and spirit since the Gothic cathedrals were built.

▶ ▶ Situating their house around a courtyard, the architects create an open home that stresses the connections between the indoors and out through light, volume, and materials. The long great room is flanked by full-height windows looking into the interior courtyard and half-height windows facing a skyline of tall trees. Concrete interior flooring flows out to the courtyard with only the glass sliding doors to separate the inside from the outside. The interior wood ceiling corresponds to the exterior wood detailing. The loft-like feeling of the great room is amplified by varying levels of windows that face views on all sides of the courtyard, neighboring park land, and San Francisco Bay.

Architecture: Donn Logan, FAIA,
    and Marcy Li Wong, AIA
Photographs: David Wakely

Formal and informal dining spaces are separated by a feature wall in this house situated on a bluff overlooking the beach. The breakfast room sits in one of the several pavilion-like spaces that radiate from the central circulation spine of the house. The freestanding divider wall separates the breakfast room from the dining room, while maintaining a sense of openness in the space. On the breakfast room side, the glass-tiled wall has functional storage space, while serving as an artistic background for the dining room.

Architecture: Ron Goldman, FAIA, Bob Firth, AIA, and Clelio Boccato, AIA
Design: James Kwan
Photographs: Charley Daniels

Stunning and brave in its starkness and complexity, this house gives extreme attention to the glass-enclosed court and lap pool. The two-story glass-fronted court acts as a protective field for the more private living and bedroom spaces. Reaching 250 feet (75 meters) out into the landscape, the glass-and-wood enclosed lap pool is a bridge to the outdoors.

Architecture: Alexander Gorlin
Photographs: Alexander Gorlin

A second-floor den is seemingly suspended within this dramatic house. The curved window-wall is delineated with wood and equipped with two operable windows. Inside, the wood-paned window wall is juxtaposed with seamless glass, which opens the space to the view below, as does the glass floor panel with view of the pool.

Architecture: Aviva Bornovski
    Carmy and Holly Bieniewski, AIA
Photographs: Douglas Hill

◄ ▼ Located in the remains of an old barn foundation on a Pennsylvania farm, this house accommodates the client's wishes for openness and privacy, as well as for rooms defined by mood and atmosphere. Planes of glass and stone work together with walls meandering in service to views and light. The contrast between ancient stone and modern glass creates a mood of both tension and intrigue.

Architecture: Peter Q. Bohlin, FAIA,
    Bernard J. Cywinski, FAIA, and
    Jon C. Jackson, AIA
Photographs: Joseph W. Molitor

This house stresses verticality in its attempt to take up as little space as possible in its natural surroundings. The dramatic entry room rises three stories, with a sitting area on the first floor, and variations on visual access on the upper floors. Views looking out are of a mature deciduous forest and Maryland's Severn River.

Architecture: Peter Q. Bohlin, FAIA, Bernard J. Cywinski, FAIA, and Jon C. Jackson, AIA
Photograph: Len Jenshel

Clever use of space allows for a greenhouse in the addition to this 160-year-old home in New England. The glass-block upper-level deck is the ceiling for the lower-level greenhouse. Additional windows are installed for greater light, while the room is bolstered by a variety of stone textures.

Architecture: McKee Patterson, AIA
Photographs: Fred George

This beach house extends outdoor living to even the most private pleasures of the bath, which is given a spectacular view of the ocean, while protected behind glass. An outdoor spa is complete with fireplace, roof covering, and plantings for privacy and warmth.

Architecture: Russell Shubin, AIA, and Timothy Morgan Steele
Photograph: Russell Shubin

Determined to create a home with a connection to the outdoors, the architects and client visited Japan to observe how buildings relate to gardens. Bedrooms and other private spaces open up to an interior courtyard, while main living spaces are encased in glass, wood, and copper pavilion-like structures. One side opens to a gravel courtyard, while the other looks upon a lush, natural garden.

Architecture: David Lake and Ted Flato
Photograph: Michael Lyon

PROTECTED PORCHES

Extending from the house, yet still encased in some sort of wall, the protected porch may be bolstered by glass, shutters, or screens. The screen affords numerous possibilities and freedom to homeowners who desire the gentle breezes and fragrances of the outdoors, but want to avoid strong winds, rain, and local fauna (bugs!).

◀ ▶ The legendary Los Angeles design icon Tony Duquette dedicated his 175-acre (70-hectare) ranch in Malibu to wondrous enchantment. The designer clearly creates a greenhouse-like space with potted plants, exotic sculptures, and island-inspired furniture. The lavish sensuality harks back to Duquette's roots in Hollywood, where he designed many sets and costumes, and counted Mary Pickford and David O. Selznick among his clients. Like Eden past, this enchanted place is no more, having burned to the ground in one of the many wildfires that plague the beauty of Malibu.

Design: Tony Duquette
Photographs: Tim Street-Porter

▲ ▲ Allowing airflow into the home, this semicircular porch is also a quiet area for reflection onto the open pasture beyond. The arcing room plays along with the geometric forms of the house—stucco-clad volumes topped with metal roofs.

Architecture: David Lake
    and Ted Flato
Photographs: Michael Lyon

The sidewalk-like path winds its way from standard-issue chain link fencing through the perfectly sewn lawn, to an abbreviated picket fence, ending at a screened-in porch with a countrified pediment entrance. The porch not only augments the existing house, but, in fact, defines it visually.

Architecture: Brian Alfred Murphy
Project Manager: Julie Hart
Photograph: Tim Street-Porter

A series of arbors alternates between open areas and screened-in porches, such as this one on a Texas ranch. Brick brings a slightly more refined ground element than the natural ground cover outside, and hand-crafted furniture adds curved elements to the angularity of the space.

Architecture: David Lake
and Ted Flato
Photograph: David Lake

▲ Three barn-like basilica structures
in varying stages of transparency—
an open steel-grid structure, one in
stone and screen, and a galvanized-
metal cladded volume—define a
home that celebrates industrial
architecture. Bounded by horizontal
screen bands, a large open space
serves as a dramatic dining room.

Architecture: David Lake
    and Ted Flato
Photograph: Undine Pröhl

◄ ▲ The architect furthers exploration of the vernacular, wood-frame designs found at the Seaside community of Florida by using elements of transparency and exaggeration. An upper-level "shutter room," designated as a secondary living space, uses floor-to-ceiling red shutters to create a private hideaway. Like the rest of the house, it is screened by contemporary lattice work that heightens the skeletal, architectural quality of the design.

Architecture: Victoria Casasco
Photographs: Victoria Casasco

OPEN DOORS

Open the door and let all of the outdoors in. That's the thought behind these rooms, where doors and windows are unified, and the line between interior and exterior is forever blurred.

Charged with creating "an old Eastern verandah" from a former recording studio, the designer uses a mix of furnishings to create space for relaxation and entertainment. Garden ornaments and topiaries mix with Neo-Classical elements for a formal, yet comfortable, space.

Design: James Blakeley, III, ASID
Photograph: Christopher Covey

▲▲ Situated in a California national forest, this weekend retreat may commonly see at least two feet (.6 meters) of winter snow. To take full advantage of the spring and summer temperatures, the architects installed glass garage doors that can be fully opened. The house is designed with the living areas on the upper level for full views of mountains and valley. Decks emerge from either side of the living room, adding further emphasis to the seamless space.

Architecture: Gwynne Pugh
    and Larry Scarpa
Photographs: Marvin Rand

▶ ▶ The architect's own home embodies southern California living and style in its insistence on equal outdoor and indoor spaces, as well as in the combination of industrial and natural materials. In the dual dining rooms, park-like outdoor furniture rests on both floors, whether they be burnished concrete or decking constructed from recycled wood forms. A translucent scrim adds privacy.

Architecture: David Hertz, AIA
Photographs: David Hertz

▲ A gentle symmetry gives this
seating area a serene feeling,
along with the bright-white
window panes, sculptural lamp,
and upholstered furniture. The
plan for this Long Island, New
York, renovation is to integrate
architecture, garden, water,
and interior.

Architecture: Lee F. Mindel, AIA
Photograph: John Murdock

▲ Nearly floor-to-ceiling glass on three sides creates a complete feeling of openness. Sliding doors lead out to a grand patio facing Florida's Intracoastal Waterway. Overscale wicker seating is upholstered in neutral colors for a light, beach-house feeling.

Architecture: Alexander Gorlin
Photograph: Steven Brooke

Dating from the 1920s, this historic Connecticut home is given a sunroom with pale green–paned, articulated window walls. Outdoor paving material is brought indoors to connect the room to the natural site.

Architecture: Lee F. Mindel, AIA
Photograph: Peter Paige

A true indoor/outdoor feeling is achieved by the tile flooring, teak furniture, and overhead fans. Varying-height doors and sidelights let in soft light from outdoors. Set for dining and relaxing, this space evokes further serenity in its monochrome tones taken from the natural teak and sisal.

Design: Joy Wolfe, ASID
Photograph: Christopher Covey

▲ Reality and illusion are at play in this octagonal breakfast room, where the designer installs French doors for physical access to the garden, along with decorative painting for more spiritual access. Other elements that bring the garden inside include wicker-and-iron furniture and an antique garden light fixture.

Design: James Kwan
Photograph: Charley Daniels

Hanging On

According to the humorous social critic Fran Lebowitz, "the outdoors is what you must pass through in order to get from your apartment into a taxicab." For homeowners today, the spaces between two forms of shelter are more than incidental atmosphere. These spaces that "hang on" to the house are celebrated and doted on. They connote leisure, luxury, and beauty. They embody our ability to tame and enjoy nature at the same time. Here, we'll look at spaces that are structurally connected to the house, yet fully intended as outdoor rooms. Porches and entries, patios and terraces, decks and balconies, and rooftops—whether in a large country manse, or a small city apartment—are vital living spaces for casual entertaining, family leisure time, or a personal respite from a busy day.

◄ ► This isolated ridge-top house features a wrap-around porch with entertainment area leading from the interior living room to the pool. Exposed wood trusses and cedar siding connect the inside and outside areas of the house. The cathedral-like archway artfully frames mountain views, further reinforcing the house's relationship to its natural surroundings and the architects' concentration on edges and openings.

Architecture: William Turnbull, Jr., and Eric Haesloop
Photographs: David Livingston

PORCHES AND ENTRIES

How you feel when you walk into your home—or how you greet guests—is a driving force behind creating pleasant, welcoming spaces for the front porch and entryway. By definition, a porch is a covered front entry, yet the form is used, of course, on all sides of a home.

▶ Turning an uninteresting, 1960s "developer special" into a traditional home more suited to its New England surroundings, the architect includes this farmhouse porch for authenticity. Traditional clapboard siding, bay windows, Colonial detailing, and contrasting trim bring the house back to the historic roots of the area. Contemporary touches, such as the open ceiling area of the porch, bring the house into today.

Architecture: David Hacin
Photograph: Rick Mandelkorn

Drama, light, and space combine in the central porch for a large Florida home. The architect combines Classicism and Modernism in the spare capitals and symmetric design. Asian-influenced furniture and objects create a sophisticated space for lounging and viewing the pool and the Intracoastal Waterway beyond.

Architecture: Alexander Gorlin
Photographs: Steven Brooke

▶ ▶ With elements of Mediterranean and Classicism, this back porch area for the architect's own home remains clean and simple. Additional architectural elements, such as the dramatic Douglas-fir roof and Spanish tile, contribute rustic interest to the porch area, which overlooks backyard and guest house. Teak furniture in comfortable proportions makes this an alternate family living room.

Architecture: John Staff, AIA
Photographs: J. Scott Smith

A drab screened-in porch is transformed into a lush garden platform, complete with tiled pond. The tile, in colors of the Mediterranean, corresponds to the feeling of the house and accents the natural colors of the plants. A stone path leads from the terrace to an outdoor seating area with a panoramic view of the garden.

Architecture: Polly Osborne, AIA, and John Erickson, AIA
Garden Design: David Chemel
Photograph: Tim Street-Porter

The deep porch off the kitchen is a bright, sunny area for dining or lounging. The architect brings warmth to the stark opening with cheerful, oversize furniture, which he designed and painted yellow.

Architecture: Roy McMakin
Photograph: Tim Street-Porter

▲ This house on Narragansett Bay in Rhode Island is sited specifically to take full advantage of the sweeping view. The broad porch is accessed from living room, dining room, kitchen, and den, emphasizing the homeowners' wishes for waterside entertaining and living spaces.

Architecture: James Estes
Photograph: Warren Jagger

▶ All the comforts of indoors are re-created in this covered porch nook, complete with fireplace and area rug. The owners, fond of the California wine country, but living in Beverly Hills, wanted rustic elements of log beams and Mediterranean tile roofing added to their otherwise Modern house.

Design: Bill Lane
Photograph: Charles S. White

▲ Bold composition and saturated
colors recall the work of Mexican
architect Luis Barragàn. Copper
cladding and irregularly cut stone
add to the rich colorations for the
entry, which sports two lounge
chairs for a quick respite.

Architecture: Steven Ehrlich, FAIA
Photograph: Alan Weintraub

▶ The porch of this showcase house is transformed into an informal study. Furniture and accessories recall world travels, while fringed exterior drapes add an element of fancy and luxury.

Design: Christine Kendall-Jent, ASID, IIDA
Photograph: Christopher Covey

◀ The architects use their own home as a continual experimentation ground to try out new ideas in outdoor living. Heightening the Mediterranean style of the house are iron accessories, ethnic furniture, and tiles—cracked and whole—embellishing tables, fireplace, and flooring.

Architecture: Brian Tichenor and Raun Thorp
Photograph: Tim Street-Porter

◄ An entry courtyard is created as a transition space between the home and the street for this beachfront property. Frosted panels and French limestone complement the stark whiteness of the architecture, and a high canopy shades the area. Cushioned banquette seating adds softness and counterpoint to the dramatic lines of the furniture.

Architecture: Arthur Erickson
Design: Barbara Barry
Photograph: Tim Street-Porter

◀ Extending from the indoor family room is a casual dining area that mixes materials of limestone, marble, steel, and aluminum. Orange trees are encased in a limestone planter-cum-fountain.

Architecture: Arthur Erickson
Design: Barbara Barry
Photograph: Tim Street-Porter

▶ This Mexican outdoor living room is covered by a large thatched palapa roof, which is supported by vine-entwined palm trunks. Fiery colors and rustic furniture add to the minimal space.

Architecture: Diego Villaseñor
Photograph: Tim Street-Porter

▼ A hidden back porch off the library and living room is the perfect spot for a quiet room. Sisal rug softens the outdoor paving. Wicker furniture gives a comfortable, lived-in feeling.

Homeowners: Larry and
    Kathryn Keele
Photograph: Mark Lohman

▲ A cozy side porch is outfitted for a Victorian tea with Nantucket-style white wicker furniture and feminine china and table accessories. Picket fence, lattice work, and plenty of climbing vines complete the charming scene.

Design: Debbie Jones
Photograph: Mark Lohman

Recalling the white walls of the Grecian isles, but having a definitely indigenous Mexican palette, this sleeping porch combines all the best motifs of coastal living. Rich Mexican hues and rough timber contrast to the delicately realized pebble sun-ray detailing on the deck.

Design: Gian Franco Brignone
Photographs: Tim Street-Porter

◄ ▲ Remodeled for a work-at-home couple with different design wishes, this split-personality house gracefully accommodates both. She wanted a New England cottage feeling, which is expressed in the wide porch, shiplap siding, and traditional details. His office and outdoor space are much more contemporary, designed with a 16-foot (5-meter) curved stucco wall and minimal wood door frames.

Architecture: Anne Troutman
Photographs: Michael Grecco

◀ ▼ A variety of porch and terrace spaces create intrigue for a 6,000-square-foot (2,000-square-meter) desert manse. Natural rock outcroppings tie the home to the land, as do the shallow horizontal steps leading to shoji-screen–like doors. Beyond the screens is a private entry court that doubles as a sculpture gallery. The poolside terrace echoes the rock-and-step patterns of the front entrance.

Architecture: David R. Olson, AIA
Photographs: Jeff O'Brien

▲ Mexico inspired these English
clothing designers to use their
house as a canvas for a palette of
exciting colors and patterns.
Blues, greens, and reds are
sponged on and wiped off, then
further worked for a weathered,
distressed look. Furniture receives
the same treatment.

Design: Michael and Hilary
   Anderson
Photograph: Tim Street-Porter

◄ ◄ Wicker seating gives a comfortable feeling to this lush porch, over which a long roof is supported by an enormous solid-wood beam from Mexico. Several distinct outdoor spaces serve different functions for the homeowners: protected lounging under the roof, spacious cooking in the open, and shaded dining on the promontory of the hillside. Slate decking is used inside the house and out, as well as along the barbecue buffet.

Design: Shepard Vineburg
Photographs: Mimi Drop

PATIOS AND TERRACES

Filled with furniture or kept minimal with expert handling of space, patios and terraces are important places for entertaining and recreation. Different paving material—slate, brick, concrete, wood—can change the mood and use of the space from formal and stark to casual and rustic.

▶ ▶ ▶ Serene and sculptural, this house for actor Ricardo Montalban is located in Hollywood but is meant to evoke Mexico. Rough plaster, vibrant colors, and sitting areas in shade and sun fulfill the requirements for both large- and small-scale entertaining. Near the dramatic and cooling pools, deep eaves create a sheltered space for concrete table and chairs (softened by cushions and pillows). Within this house, the architect is continually playing with notions of protection and exposure. A broad, bright terrace boldly faces the city of Los Angeles with its rough, ochre-colored plaster, Mexican tile floor, and cactus plantings that defy the elements.

Architecture: Ricardo Legorreta
Photographs: Mary E. Nichols

A sheltered pool and extensive outdoor entertaining area are highlighted by the architect's customary rough-plaster finishes and brilliant colors. The contrast between indoor and outdoor is further heightened in this desert home by areas of deep shade and bright sunlight. The building itself is designed to blend into the landscape, as a simple wall on the crest of a hill.

Architecture: Ricardo Legorreta
Photograph: Lourdes Legorreta

Living room, dining room, kitchen, and sitting area are all accommodated on the expansive terrace of this beachfront property. Concrete pavers separate the house from the sand and echo the dominant material used in constructing the terrace. Glass panels protect the owners from the elements while maintaining the transparency that is so important in this home. A curved upper deck is cantilevered over the sitting area, providing shade for the area below as well as additional outdoor space for the private family areas on the second floor. The unique surfacing of the deck comprises metal grating with glass overlay.

Architecture: David Lawrence
    Gray, FAIA
Photographs: Tim Street-Porter

▲ The noted Japanese architect Arata
Isozaki creates an outdoor gallery
for a house and studio, just one
block from the California beach.
Visitors pass through the broad
expanse of concrete to enter this
skylit house for an art collector, who
uses the terrace as a year-round
dining room. A water sculpture and
lush environmental art combine
with cactus and concrete in a dual
comparison of water and land.

Architecture: Arata Isozaki
Photograph: Tom Bonner

Flexible use of space—and low-cost living—were the ideas behind the original architecture for this 1948 house by California Modernist Gregory Ain. The current architect/homeowner updates the space with a primary-color palette, partially covered terrace, and three distinct garden areas within a small outdoor plot. Easy-to-maintain materials include redwood decking, Arizona red sandstone pavers, and custom-colored concrete.

Architecture: Richard Corsini
Photographs: Anthony Pinto

A 2,000-square-foot (180-square-meter) terrace radiates from the interior breakfast area, kitchen, and family room, creating corresponding areas outdoors. Teak furniture with neutral upholstery blend with the house's concrete-and-wood color scheme.

Architecture: Mark D. Kirkhart, AIA, and William S. Wolf
Photograph: Christopher Covey

▶ A fabric canopy shades one seating area on this pool patio, while another area is defined by a glass-block niche. Plays of transparency abound in use of glass block, glazed and unglazed openings, and scrims.

Architecture: Bernardo Fort-Brescia, FAIA, and Laurinda Hope Spear, FAIA
Photograph: Tim Street-Porter

▼ Dealing with a narrow lot and high-rise neighboring buildings, the architect opts for a central courtyard with dining and spa areas. The kitchen opens out to the green Vermont slate paving, which adds to other weatherproof materials, such as water-sealed fir, resin-finished marine plywood, and stucco, to withstand the ocean air.

Architecture: Anne Troutman
Photograph: Grey Crawford

◄ ◄ Perched on a sloping site, this
Los Angeles home artfully
accommodates space in its
planning and design. The pool is
protected by the upper level of the
house, which is cut with skylight
openings. Because it's tucked
farther in, the seating area can be
given indoor finishes of wood and
metal, and accessories such as area
rugs. A built-in bench/bar at the
end of the pool adds a rich wood
tone to the play of subtle light and
coloring in this space.

Architecture: Aviva Bornovski
   Carmy and Holly Bieniewski, AIA
Photographs: Douglas Hill

Decks and Balconies

Elevated above the ground or cantilevered from the building, decks and balconies provide unique vantage points. Many are used as small meditation spots, with just a simple chair or two, while others are full-scale living and dining rooms.

▶ Decks abound in this architects' house configured around a central courtyard. Keeping with the purity of Modernist design, the deck comprises its essential elements. The space, however, is protected and intimate with the addition of a slatted-wood covering that relates to the shading structures attached to the house itself. Seen from the courtyard below, the deck blends seamlessly into the house's exterior, using the same stone, wood, and metal patterns and materials.

Architecture: Donn Logan, FAIA, and Marcy Li Wong, AIA
Photograph: David Wakely

The back deck of a beachfront cottage is nearly one-third of the house's footprint. The open roof mimics the broad overhanging eaves of the main structure and gives partial shade from the Florida sun. Detail in furniture and lighting is kept minimal.

Architecture: Alexander Gorlin
Photograph: Steven Brooke

With great architecture to begin with, this 1949 house by Los Angeles Modernist icon Richard Neutra is enhanced by the architect/owner with a galvanized steel container running opposite the low stucco wall to further enclose the private deck. The line between indoor and outdoor disappears when the large sliding-glass doors are opened. The outdoor furniture is also designed by Neutra.

Architecture: Daniel Sachs
Photograph: Tim Street-Porter

◀ ◀ Designed in the tradition of California Modernism, this spectacular house is replete with indoor/outdoor spaces intended for entertainment and casual living. Sliding glass doors allow for a seamless flow between living room and deck. Modernist furniture indoors and outdoors further blurs the distinction between inside and outside.

Architecture: Hagy Belzberg
Photographs: Tim Street-Porter

▲ The architects respond to the site and natural conditions for this house on the Connecticut shore. The upper-level deck is connected to a covered porch and dining terrace on lower levels by a single staircase. Weathered planks and glass blocks stand up to the elements.

Architecture: David E. Austin, AIA, and Dana Marcu
Photograph: Dan Cornish

◀ Nestled in a mountain valley, this house was built with the environment in mind, both in its siting and use of materials. Clean architectural lines create a seamless flow between living room and side deck.

Architecture: Russell Shubin, AIA, and Robin Donaldson, AIA
Photograph: Farshid Assassi

▶ A small bedroom deck overlooks a courtyard space below. Douglas fir, water sealed for protection from the elements, is used for both horizontal and vertical emphasis, as well as for its rich color and contrast to gray stucco.

Architecture: Anne Troutman
Photograph: Grey Crawford

▼ Serpentine walls echo each others' forms, creating a marble-paved area overlooking a pool below. Indigenous stone from Mallorca, Spain, clads the wall surfaces in a vertical pattern, giving contrast to the broad horizontal geometry.

Architecture: Victoria Casasco and Carlos Garcia Delgado
Photograph: Lourdes Jansana

For their own house, the architects created four separate decks (south, east, west, and roof), each of minimal design, capturing the essence and quiet of simple form. The entry deck is partially covered by one arm of an L-shape, which is the dominant motif in the design of the house. Seemingly piercing the wall, the canopy is clad with corrugated aluminum for the exterior and birch plywood inside.

Architecture: Hideaki Ariizumi and Glynis M. Berry
Photographs: Paul Warchol

◄ Spectacular views can be seen from this house with multi-level outdoor rooms, from the pool-side recreation room, to the cantilevered balcony and master suite den. Graphic architectural lines form the triangular balcony spit, which suspends the occupant within the dramatic view.

Architecture: Joe Addo
Photograph: Erhard Pfeiffer

▶ A small space can reap great rewards with a little attention and strategic choices. A simple, yet effective, sitting area lets the homeowners converse privately, as well as take in the surrounding skyscape. Low-maintenance plants and furniture allow the space to be used year-round with little upkeep and bother.

Architecture: David Hertz, AIA
Photograph: Tom Bonner

▶ ▶ Backed against the forest but facing the ocean, this beach house is used as a company retreat by the firm that built it. Front and back walls of windows afford views from both decks, through the house, and into nature. An expansive back deck runs up against the forest hillside; the smaller front deck overlooks the Oregon coast.

Architecture: Stanley Boles, Kevin Johnson, and John O'Toole
Photographs: Laurie Black

▲ The wonderful climate of Santa Barbara, California, allows this homeowner to use the second-floor balcony as his main dining area. The Spanish Mission flavor of the city is maintained in the distressed beams, terra-cotta flooring, specially made tiles, and iron furniture and lighting fixtures that maintain the style of the 1925 house.

Homeowner: Bob Morris
Photograph: Christopher Covey

▶ ▶ A glass room opens to the outdoor
deck through 9-foot (2.7-meter)
doors that provide fine-tuned
control over the amount of breeze
allowed into the room. Mullions,
fretwork, and trellises add elegant
strength to the space.

Architecture: Lise Claiborne
    Matthews, AIA, ASID
Photographs: Grey Crawford

Traditional indoor elements of cushions, fireplace, and sleeping areas are brought outside for the double-level outdoor living space in the architect's own home. The structure is created from Hertz's invention Syndecrete, a synthetic, environmentally friendly concrete-like material. Although hard and industrial gray, the material is softened by 100-percent natural cotton upholstery and wicker seating in the traditional material of rattan. Interior and exterior woodwork in Douglas fir unifies the two spaces.

Architecture: David Hertz, AIA
Photographs: Tim Street-Porter (top); Tom Bonner (bottom)

A quarter-circle balcony is accessible from a spiral staircase on the outside and from the master suite on the inside. The open space is carved out of a previously closed-in room, with steel beams replacing the torn-down walls. A metal trellis overhead adds to the dynamic geometry of the design.

Architecture: Ron Goldman, FAIA, Bob Firth, AIA, and Clelio Boccato, AIA
Photographs: Ron Goldman

◀ Beyond the doors, a small deck is cantilevered out from the master bedroom. Concrete walls almost converge in space, but are separated by a glass panel that lets in the pine forest view.

Architecture: David Hertz, AIA
Photograph: David Hertz

◀ A simple balcony is given dramatic emphasis with the rich colorations and deep tones of the stucco and wood. The shallow eave allows for plays of both brightness and shadow.

Architecture: Aviva Bornovski
    Carmy and Holly Bieniewski, AIA
Photograph: Douglas Hill

▲ A comfortable cottage feeling is
achieved with wicker furniture,
various floral prints, throw pillows,
and white picket railing. Both
designer and photographer live in
this house, which has several
garden spaces.

Design: Janet Lohman
Photograph: Mark Lohman

▲ The designer uses flea-market
finds and old fabrics for a lived-in,
low-maintenance, cozy look for her
own home. This breakfast area is off
the kitchen of a 1940s cottage-style
house, which the designer referred
to as a "park pavilion" because of
its closeness to nature and the
occasional hummingbird visitor.

Design: Sandy Koepke
Photograph: Mark Lohman

ROOFTOPS

What greater freedom is there, than opening up one's home to the sky? City houses with roof access are highly coveted, and the rooftops are frequently adorned to create sparkling oases. More natural landscape can be seen from rooftops that are made comfortable for stargazing and communing with the big sky.

◄ Supported by Doric columns, a vine-covered pergola helps divide a tight, Manhattan penthouse terrace into sitting and dining areas. Brick-colored pavers slyly correspond to the brick buildings surrounding it, while the gray pergola echoes the beautifully weathered redwood furniture.

Design: Noel Jeffrey
Photograph: Peter Vitale

▲ Bright upholstery and many plants
in terra-cotta pots add color and
verve to a secluded roof deck.
The designer adds seating space
by transforming one side of
the perimeter railing into a
long banquette.

Design: Debbie Jones
Photograph: Mark Lohman

◀ ▶ Paned doors lead to the simple roof deck. Weathered wood and rough plaster play counterpoint to the New Orleans French Quarter moldings and balustrade. A spiral staircase leads to the very top, where a hot tub and views of the community await.

Architecture: Alexander Gorlin
Photographs: Michael Moran

▶ A sunbathing roof is equipped with over-stuffed cushions on custom metal chaise lounges. The balustrade is topped with mirrored balls that reflect sunlight and scenery.

Design: Sarah Boyer Jenkins, FASID, and Edward Wesely
Photograph: Gordon Beall

BREAKING FREE

What makes a room a room? Many people would say that a room contains at least one wall. But we are interested in spaces that defy such definitions. Just as it's not the structure that makes a house a home, it's not walls that make a space a room. Intimacy and intent are paramount criteria. Intimacy may be achieved in the grand outdoors by the furniture type and placement. Plants, ground cover, arbors, and trellises all contribute to create spaces that suggest comfort and feelings of freedom in the outdoors.

In Charles Baudelaire's imaginary garden, "There is nothing else but grace and measure,/Richness, quietness, and pleasure." For many homeowners, a beautiful garden space need not be imagined. By working with designers, architects, and landscapers who understand the terrain, you can enjoy quietness and pleasure in your own home.

◄ ▶ A vast courtyard separates the glass-fronted main house from the guest house, and is flanked on either side by manifestations of water. The quiet lap pool on one side contrasts with the intriguing stairway on the other. Inset ponds with river rocks are a metaphor for a tranquil stream flowing to the sea.

Architecture: David Lawrence Gray, FAIA
Photographs: Tim Street-Porter

COURTYARDS

Though bound by the walls of the house, well-designed courtyards evoke dual feelings of containment and expansion. While formal courtyards may be used for high-end entertaining, many West Coast homeowners use their courtyards as year-round dining—and even conference—spaces.

◀ Log beams on one side and trees on the other bolster this small, yet effective, space. Stone flooring creates a surface peninsula that supports the wrought-iron breakfast seating set. Rather than extend the stone to the stucco wall, the designer includes a grassy area, which effectively makes the garden passage seem larger and also defines a separate area for casual dining.

Design: Bill Lane
Photograph: Charles S. White

A two-part courtyard acts as a unifying space for this dual-structure home, with the gatehouse toward the front of the property, and the principal residence in the back with a southern exposure. Alternating plaster colors and different paving set the spaces apart, while the green trim throughout holds the look together.

Architecture: Mark Mack
Photographs: Tim Street-Porter

◄ ◄ A colorful courtyard serves as dining and meeting space for the home and studio of graphic designer Charlie Hess, who, working closely with landscape designer Mayita Dinos, transforms a dirt pit into redwood-and-mosaic oasis. A brave mix of colors and materials, such as Mexican tile, pebbles, terra-cotta pavers, redwood, and painted and weathered teak, bring energy to a relatively small space.

Design: Charlie Hess and Mayita Dinos
Photographs: Tim Street-Porter

▲ Rustic austerity describes this
remodel of a 1950s A-frame by the
owners/designers. Timber furniture
and rough-hewn stone contribute
to the rural French farmhouse style.
The courtyard has sweeping views
of the ocean, yet is made cozy by
the outdoor fireplace.

Design: John O'Neill and James Palmer
Photograph: Christopher Covey

▲ The designer brings Spanish
Colonial Revival to her own home in
an expansive courtyard, complete
with fireplace, banquettes, and
several sitting and dining areas.
Early California artifacts, and her
own furniture designs, bring warmth
and intimacy to the large space.

Design: Kathleen Spiegelman
Photograph: Tim Street-Porter

▶ Several spaces on the brick-paved
courtyard are defined by their
furniture: a wicker deep-seating
group fosters long conversations;
antique wicker uprights form a
cozy tête-à-tête; a metal table
and chairs accommodate casual
dining; lounge chairs are protected
within the mock-Tudor porch;
and simple benches call for
solitary contemplation.

Design: Barbara Barry
Photograph: Tim Street-Porter

▶ The designer and photographer use the courtyard as a year-round dining room in their Hollywood Hills home, former manse of the famed costume designer Adrian. Strategic plantings, fireplace, and nearby fountain add charm and elegance.

Design: Annie Kelly
Photograph: Tim Street-Porter

◀ Creativity knows no bounds for the husband-and-wife design team who create a lush, cottage-like outdoor room in a 1930s Los Angeles housing complex. Where once was fake grass, now are terra-cotta pavers and a multitude of potted flowers and greenery. French bistro chairs add a delicate touch.

Architecture: Odom Stamps
Design: Kate Stamps
Photograph: Tim Street-Porter

A banal lawn is transformed into an enchanted water room with lush koi pond and dining area. The bright colors echo the citrus trees as well as the Bauer pottery used as the fountain font. Mosaic table is by artist Nancy Kintisch.

Landscape Architecture: Rob Steiner

Photographs: Steven A. Gunther

▲ Elegant, Italian Renaissance–
inspired furniture groups border
a formal area designed for
entertaining. Contemplative
sculpture is a focal point, and
stone garden ornaments enhance
the stately, yet inviting, space.

Design: Sarah Boyer Jenkins,
    FASID, and Edward Wesley
Photograph: Gordon Beall

▶ Bedroom, living room, and dining room form the walls of an outdoor living/dining room in the renovated home for landscape architect Rob Pressman. Concrete pavers are grouted with grass; broad steps leading down to the space double as amphitheater-like seating. The fireplace brings added warmth to the space.

Architecture: Jeffrey Michael Tohl
Landscape Architecture: Rob
    Pressman
Photograph: Michael Arden

◀ Carved out of a three-bedroom, hillside house, a simple courtyard provides hard- and soft-scape areas for the family. Living spaces open on the courtyard, which, like the rest of the house, is conceived from simple, yet elegant, materials.

Architecture: Gwynne Pugh
    and Larry Scarpa
Photograph: Larry Scarpa

A courtyard is visible through large windows in the entrance foyer, which separates two wings of the house. Rich ochre tones and wooden details are used to evoke the casual, yet vibrant, lifestyles of Napa Valley and Tuscany. The small, Romeo-and-Juliet balcony adds charm and whimsy.

Design: Gary Orr
Photographs: Jay Graham

TRELLISES

Arbors and trellises add a certain romance and Classicism to an outdoor space. The often-simple wood structures rein in an area and bring formality to processions and patios.

▲ ▶ A long arbor extends over the brick path from the pool, leading to the spa grotto. The spa is open to the sky, while side areas, paved with colored concrete, are screened by grape and wisteria on the arbor. Delicately intertwined metal furniture echoes the natural growth patterns of the overhead vines.

Design: Gary Orr
Photographs: Jay Graham

▲ Colored stucco columns support
the trellis that casts dramatic
shadows onto a bar-equipped
entertainment space. Irregularly
sized Idaho stone defines the
space within the rest of the lawn-
covered yard.

Architecture: Steven Ehrlich, FAIA
Photograph: Alan Weintraub

◀ ◀ Wooden trusses supported by terra-cotta columns define several areas of an expansive outdoor suite, which is fully transformed from a bland ranch-house exterior. Multilevel terraces paved in terra cotta and colored concrete accommodate entertaining and family dining. Built-in barbecue and fireplace further contribute to the use and flexibility of the space.

Design: Gary Orr
Photographs: Jay Graham

GARDEN ROOMS

The most amorphous of room spaces are those that are set in gardens, with only natural elements and furnishings to define the space. Not merely gardens with benches, these outdoor rooms truly embrace warmth, intimacy, and design.

▶ ▶ Steel-and-teak furniture creates a serpentine counterpart to the square pavers for an energetic garden that lies between two, three-story buildings connected by a catwalk. A rock-garden border surrounds concrete pavers, with moss growing between the lines. The space is bordered by walls of steel, doors of white-painted pegboard and white acrylic sheeting, and sliding panels of medium-density fiberboard and acrylic sheeting.

Design: Sallie Trout
Photographs: Tom Bonner

▲ Potted and planted succulents
abound amid cactus-colored metal
chairs and tile-top table. The simple
placement of plants and furniture
creates a space for reflection.

Architecture: Roy McMakin
Photograph: Tim Street-Porter

▶ The designer creates a lush garden fantasy for his own home with climbing roses and moss hiding a wooden gazebo. Refined iron furniture contrasts with a rustic twig chair.

Design: Stephen Suzman
Photograph: Jerry Harpur

▼ Situated within a "ruined landscape," as the designer describes it, are several small seating areas. A fragmented wall appears to be the remains of a former structure, yet is newly designed and placed. This artistic display of water, stone, and flowers gives way to a more ordered patio.

Design: Gary Orr
Photograph: Jay Graham

This 40-foot by 80-foot (12.2 meter by 24.4-meter) area is coined "the empty room" by the architect and homeowner for its simple definition of space bound on one side by a low, dry-mortar stone wall and on the other by a Richard Serra steel sculpture. The clean emptiness—ideal for contemplative afternoons—is even maintained with the addition of badminton space that is planted with a different type of sod to delineate the court area.

Landscape Architect: Pamela Burton
Photographs: Allan Mandell

POOL SURROUNDS

The pool is a perfect example of captured nature—a pond of one's own, if you will. There is much more variety of shape and color in today's pools, and equal, if not greater, attention is paid to the areas surrounding them.

▲ The feelings of enclosure and protection are afforded by the spa pavilion of yellow and blue plaster. The open pool area is buttressed by the concrete bench along the water, and the garden wall, which stops the space from flowing into the landscape.

Architecture: Ricardo Legorreta
Photograph: Lourdes Legorreta

◄ ▲ Distinctions between sky, sea, and
land disappear. A sky-blue pool is
redesigned to overflow the cliff's
edge and seemingly blend with the
Pacific Ocean. The patio, surfaced
with blue-green-gray concrete, is
bound by low concrete seating
walls and planted with succulents
chosen for their dramatic profiles
as well as their low maintenance.

Landscape Architecture:
    Pamela Burton
Photographs: John Reed Forsman

◀ ▲ Narrow space necessitates creativity in the design and installation of this Tuscan-inspired pool and patio area in the Hollywood Hills. High walls on either side maintain a soft yellow color that corresponds with the stone paving, creating a delicate and open feeling. Stone planters, an Italianate fountain, and an ornamental obelisk give the feeling of a grand European garden, as does the tamed, trellised ivy and neatly manicured shrubs.

Design: Mark Warwick
    and Kim Hoffman
Photographs: Patrick House

Melding into the earth tones of the Arizona desert, this strong, massive house presents its pool and outdoor room area as a place of further calm and contemplation. Bright desert hues of fuchsia and aqua are used sparingly, but to great effect, in the spa- and pool-tile detailing. A series of horizontal planes creates the illusion of a stacked horizon of water, wall, and mountain. A structure affording daytime shade, evening light, and heat relief rises above the informal dining area.

Architecture: David Hacin
Photographs: Chuck Choi

▼ Rustic, yet refined, twig and woven furniture defines several separate dining and seating areas. Twin pool-side dining pavilions are draped with muslin and support candle-filled iron chandeliers.

Design: Chip Kalleen, IIDA
Photograph: Dan Francis

The designer's weekend home is an example of refined style. The square pool sits within its platform in a neat, geometric layout, almost like an Josef Albers painting. This quiet homage to the square gets energy from the many-hued fieldstone surrounding the pool. A continuity of materials is gained by using the same stone around the house. A casual, trellised breakfast area is just beyond the kitchen window.

Design: Vicente Wolf
Photographs: Vicente Wolf

▲ A stark stucco wall with large
punched-out openings forms a
dramatic backdrop for a hillside spa
and seating area. Circular spa and
irregularly shaped stones play in
counterpoint to the strict angular
geometry of the house and furniture.

Architecture: Ron Goldman, FAIA,
Bob Firth, AIA, and Clelio
Boccato, AIA
Photograph: Derek Rath

◄ One of several entertainment
terraces, the pool level sports a
rich, monochromatic scheme in the
flagstone, iron furniture, and deep
taupe upholstery. Distinct areas
form dining room, living room, and
sitting area on this terrace that is
equipped with sophisticated
sound equipment.

Design: Susan Jay Freeman, ASID
Photograph: Christopher Covey

▲▶ The designer furnishes the outdoor space of her own home with creative use of raw materials: poured concrete legs support a black-granite table top; smooth concrete flooring is interrupted by pool and pebbles; stained concrete benches provide seating and separation of vegetation area; charcoal-stained concrete-block bar supports a slate top; and natural concrete-block wall frames the yard. With the owner's two dogs enjoying the yard, planting grass was not an option, so the designer opts for gravel and pebbles.

Design: Raquel Vert
Photographs: Eric Staudenmaier

▲ A bold, white-stucco wall, which
acts as a backdrop to the outdoor
dining room, creates a picture
frame for the mountains. Taking the
idea of a pool house to another
dimension, the designer cantilevers
a metal-mesh awning from the wall,
creating shade and protection from
sun and wind. Redwood deck,
concrete water fountain, grass
inserts, and free-form rocks add to
the geometric play.

Design: Ilan Dei
Photograph: Dircum Over

◄ ◄ A stucco-and-timber trellis defines
the terrace of a Mexican-inspired
Los Angeles home. The outdoor
pool area is the first vista seen by
visitors as they walk through the
glass-enclosed entry cube. The
design of the house is shaped by
dramatic rock formations and
layered mountain ranges. Intense
earth colors mirror the landscape
and the sunsets around this house
that sits so naturally in its site.

Architecture: Ron Goldman, FAIA,
    Bob Firth, AIA, and Clelio
    Boccato, AIA
Photographs: Undine Pröhl

INSIDE OUT

A room outdoors can consist of four walls with an optional roof. It may have a roof with barely a hint of wall holding it up. Sometimes these rooms are stark, almost sculptural, and other times playful, harking back to the tradition of architectural follies. Others are decked out in full regalia, plush as the great indoors. All, however, are true outdoor rooms—single spaces that can be defined architecturally in the outdoors.

These spaces fulfill several functions. They may be strictly ornamental—a pretty pavilion in the garden. Often they are designed to complement the pool, servicing swimmers while providing shelter away from the house. Free from the constraints of the main house, single-room structures allow designers and architects greater freedom to experiment and express themselves in design, materials, and construction.

◀ ▶ The designer creates a serene green retreat for her own Hollywood Hills home. A thatched trellis roof covers an outdoor dining room with a painted green interior and green-and-white furniture. A large mirror gives the illusion of more space by reflecting the dining room and the outdoor spaces beyond. The covered intimacy of the space allows the designer to use fine china and silver outdoors.

Design: Barbara Barry
Photographs: Sally Gall

RETREATS

A private retreat, apart from the main house, allows
psychological as well as physical separation from the every day.
Used for reading, meditation, or work, these spaces are special
to their owners for their ability to restore and refresh.

◀ ▲ ▶ This exquisite and daring outdoor folly reinterprets a Mexican walled garden in a series of boxes, gardens within gardens, and mysterious passageways, creating, in the words of the designer, "a metaphor of a house." Saturated colors and selected cacti heighten the desert atmosphere in this art/contemplation area, which is situated within an existing lush English-style garden in Texas. This project stretches the definitions of space, room, and garden. Rooms are filled only with space, while gardens are art galleries.

Design: Martha Schwartz
Photographs: Tim Harvey

Translucence and opacity are playfully combined in a greenhouse/garage on the architects' own property. Plastic sheets cover a wood-frame structure on the roof and two sides. The other two sides are made of wood, with windows in translucent plastic. The plastic walls are humorously equipped with opaque windows.

Architecture: Hideaki Ariizumi and
    Glynis M. Berry
Photographs: Studio A/B

◄ Playfully called "Jabba the Hut" by the owner/architect, this 8-foot (2.5-meter) square room was designed with laminated glass, Douglas fir, redwood shingles, and copper siding. Front and back doors are made of four movable panels to provide variable ventilation options and allow the room to be as transparent as possible.

Architecture: Aleks Istanbullu
Photograph: Fred Stocker

PAVILIONS AND GAZEBOS

Flirting with mass, the trellis and fretwork of a delicate garden pavilion rejoices in openness. Ready-made gazebos are easily personalized with favorite furniture, while a custom design can often stand alone as a stark and mysterious structure.

▶ Designed as a vista view from the main house balcony, this intimate garden space is outfitted with a steeply pitched shingle-roof gazebo, highlighted by a finial from the owner, a garden antiques dealer. White iron furniture contributes to the light, graceful feeling inside the gazebo, while a rustic, twig-inspired iron bench rests on the herringbone brick patio.

Design: Stephen Suzman
Photograph: Jerry Harpur

▼ ▶ A string of potted citrus trees leads
to two intersecting semicircular
volumes—one of Bouquet Canyon
stone, the other of white steel
framework—that provide a seating
and contemplation area in this
artistically designed vegetable
garden. The stone retaining wall
serves as a waterfall, allowing a
continual flow of water to seep
through the cracks. The vegetable
plot is sectioned into discreet
units, stratified into different levels.

Architecture: Michael Palladino
Landscape Architecture:
    Pamela Burton
Photographs: Allan Mandell

◄ ▲ Built as a retreat for the architect and friends just outside Joshua Tree National Monument in the California desert, this remarkable structure includes a geometric gazebo painted in the burnt orange of desert blooms. Openings of irregular shapes in the stucco walls frame views of the high desert.

Architecture: Josh Schweitzer
Photographs: Tom Bonner

◄ ▲ A steel-frame hexagon trellis wrapped with a forty-year-old vine forms the ceiling for an entertainment gazebo with a city view. The concrete floor is finished for a terrazzo look, and the fireplace is clad with rough, high-desert stone. The bar counter is clad with copper and topped with stainless steel.

Architecture: Lise Claiborne
    Matthews, AIA, ASID
Photographs: Grey Crawford

▲ A formal garden gazebo is the focal
point for breakfast, afternoon tea,
or entertaining. The owners replace
a wooden floor with a sunburst
brick pattern, and furnish the space
with all-weather wicker seating.

Homeowners: Larry and Kathryn
    Keele
Photograph: Mark Lohman

▶ Santa Rita stone and grass replace
concrete decking around the pool,
which is situated at the lower level of
a sloping lot. The pergola provides a
shaded reading and resting area by
the pool and a visual resting point
from the upper-level terraces and
the country club beyond.

Architecture: Brian Tichenor and
    Raun Thorp
Photograph: Tim Street-Porter

◄▲ A garden pavilion's raised-deck flooring—complete with painted rug—and dropped-canvas ceiling add greater illusion to the interior hand-painted canvas panels. Carved redwood furniture repeats flora and fauna motifs found in the fabrics, accessories, and wall paintings. Full-height curtained openings leading to a stone balustrade, and the canvas-backed lattice work, contribute to the play of indoor and outdoor.

Design: Albert Janz, IIDA, and Sherry Stein
Photographs: Grey Crawford

POOL HOUSES

Our national monuments are reflected by water, so why not our own homes? Pool houses offer estate-like vistas as well as warm shelter after a relaxing dip.

▶ ▶ ▶ Set deep into the slope of the hillside, this sandstone-faced pool house includes a bath, sauna, and roof-top terrace. The rough-hewn, yet tightly constructed, stone pool-surround, platform, and steps leading to the pool house correspond with the lighter texture sandstone and teak pocket doors. Within the main pool house space, the stone flooring continues in the stark, meditative room whose concrete ceiling is dotted with glass cylinders through which a pattern of light passes. Emphasizing its placement in the hill slope, the pool house's side steps lead to the roof deck.

Architecture: Susan Narduli, AIA
Landscape Architecture:
    Pamela Burton
Photographs: Fred Stocker

◀ ▲ The pool house for the noted fashion designer Adrienne Vittadini is a rich dramatic setting made comfortable with lush drapes and upholstered furniture. The architect combines English garden tradition with Italian country design, including hints of Palladian and Shingle-style architecture.

Architecture: Alexander Gorlin
Photographs: Ed Addeo

◄ ▼ Belying its East Coast location, this traditional and stately pool house has whimsical and unexpected touches in its fountain frond finials and mischievous squirrel ornament. Exterior curtains and welcoming decorative lintel lead the visitor into the exquisite and mannered interior. Mixing wrought-iron furniture from the 1940s with a nineteenth-century French campaign bed and Empire mirror, the designer combines comfort, whimsy, and elegance.

Design: Noel Jeffrey
Photographs: Mick Hales

▲ Lattice work and formal garden structure contribute to this poolside pavilion. Wicker furniture, lush fabrics, and plenty of accessories bring warmth and comfort to the backyard hideaway.

Design: Joseph Ruggiero
Photograph: Tim Street-Porter

Set in a private arboretum, this indoor pool is connected to a Victorian residential complex by extended concrete walls. A serpentine stone wall contrasts with the angularly articulated glass and aluminum walls for an indoor pool. The irregularly shaped pool evokes a tamed river and continues outside to the fern-filled glen. Constant plays of contradictions—inside/outside, mechanical/natural, solid/liquid—abound in this remarkable structure.

Architecture: Peter Q. Bohlin, FAIA,
    Bernard J. Cywinski, FAIA, and
    Jon C. Jackson, AIA
Photographs: Karl A. Backus

FILLING UP

A revolution has occurred in modern furniture with the emphasis on more casual living. These days, outdoor spaces are furnished with as much attention as those indoors. Manufacturers are designing and producing materials in sophisticated styles resulting in investment-quality furniture. Indoor/outdoor qualities are important, too, as homeowners desire flexibility and value.

▶ Architectural columns add to the Neo-Classical flavor of the Empress arm chair, designed by John Caldwell for The Veneman Collection, and evoke early nineteenth-century Empire-style furniture.

◀ Knoll presents PaperClip café tables created by Vignelli Designs as a companion to the classic Bertoia side chair, both exhibiting lightness of form and graphic lines.

Photograph: Michael Arden

Historical

Pairing two legendary Italian eras, Capital Garden Products presents the Medici Vase on the Pompeii Pedestal, which resemble ancient stone but are fabricated from fiberglass.

From Classical to Neo-Classical, historical styles are ever popular in outdoor furniture and accessories. Victorian and Nantucket motifs are traditional for outdoors, but designers are turning to ancient, Renaissance, and nineteenth-century styles as well.

Hand-carved chair and side table of redwood with a silvery weathered finish from Reed Bros. Europa Collection add European elegance to the garden.

Harking back to early nineteenth-century campaign furniture, John Kelly designs a folding umbrella chair that allows for rest and shade anywhere one travels.

Haddonstone's Corinthian column well head is manufactured in the tradition of English garden ornaments but uses specially treated and cast reconstructed limestone.

Venus (from Sandro Botticelli's masterpiece) is interpreted in tile mosaic by artist Annie Sabroux, who creates custom, site-specific works.

A nineteenth-century French olive jar is reproduced by The Elegant Earth and given a mottled patina to simulate age and use.

Fifty pieces comprise the Renaissance collection designed by Enrique Gamboa in cast aluminum with antique finishes by Terra Furniture.

Neo-Classical styling with Spanish overtones informs the design of the Isabella collection in cast aluminum by John Caldwell for Tropitone.

▲ Exuding Edwardian charm, this bench, a replica of one designed by Sir Edwin Lutyens in the early 1900s for the gardens at Sissinghurst Castle, is offered today by Barlow Tyrie in plantation-grown teak.

▲ Intricate Aegean mosaic area rugs from Ann Sacks Tile & Stone are designed by Ellen Williamson and made from naturally colored and shaped stones.

▲ French artist Jacques Lamy harks back to Neo-Classical shapes for his collection of benches, urns, and pedestals from Archiped Classics in cast stone, with bronze components.

▲ Cathedral arches are shaped in wrought aluminum for the Gothic two-seater bench from McKinnon and Harris.

ROMANTIC

Flowers and baskets, swooping graceful lines, and traditional styles bring romance and lazy summer days to mind. Outdoors is where wonder and imagination are expressed best through wicker and wood.

▼ Delicate candle sconces are offered by The Elegant Earth, which reproduces the design from a nineteenth-century French original.

▲ Abstracted flowers, drooping petals, and gilt accents define Flora dinnerware by Ann Morhauser of Annieglass in slumped glass painted white for a porcelain-like effect.

Photograph: R. J. Muna

▶ A classic ocean liner steamer with solid brass fittings, made by Kingsley-Bate, adjusts to four positions and folds for compact storage.

▲ This Ram's Head urn by Capital Garden Products is made of lightweight fiberglass that is imbedded with bronze powder to effect a natural patina finish.

▲ Painterly illusion abounds in Annie Sabroux's custom tile mural that brings beauty and depth to an outdoor niche.

▲ This charming flower basket with haut relief along the rim is made of Haddonstone's reconstituted limestone, which is tested and treated for outdoor endurance.

▼ Weatherend's Quarter Circle settee is inspired by furniture found at a turn-of-the-century Maine coast estate and is updated using marine-grade paint on mahogany.

▲ The Front Porch collection from Lloyd/Flanders presents all the traditional charm of wicker furniture in its noted all-weather wicker made from paper-wrapped woven wires dipped in weatherproof coating.

▲ Sonoma, designed John Caldwell for Tropitone, presents grapevine and leaf motifs in cast aluminum.

◀ The Sun Deck adjustable stacking chaise from Summit Furniture is infused with grace and style by yacht stylist John Munford.

▲ The Essex tea trolley from Windsor Designs is made from Shorea wood, a mahogany-like hardwood that is stronger, heavier, and more plentiful than teak.

► The Eastlake collection by Brown Jordan evokes lazy days associated with wicker furniture but has a modern twist—the wicker is constructed from resin imbedded with ultraviolet inhibitors.

◀ Traditional construction techniques and modern technology come together in the Glenham circular tree seat from Barlow Tyrie, made of plantation-grown, all-weather teak that is cut to shape, rather than bent or steamed.

▲ Mottahedeh offers Tulip earthenware plates, cups, and saucers reproduced from originals in the Museum of Decorative Arts, Paris.

◀ Graceful curves abound in Lawrence Peabody's Gatsby design for Terra Furniture made of cast aluminum.

RUSTIC

Timber and twig furniture truly form a connection with nature. Rustic looks also include materials such as stone and reclaimed barnwood. Some manufacturers even offer the illusion of rustication in clever designs and materials.

▲ Naturally weathered wood is used to make Frontier Barnwood's Strong Box planter.

▲ The classic Adirondack chair—this one from Richardson Allen—continues to be an all-time favorite for its deep seating comfort and relaxed look.

◄ The simple, honest form of these Long Toms is derived from nineteenth-century tomato pots and is made today in English terra cotta by Kinsman Company.

▲ Through state-of-the-art graphic technology, Imagine Tile produces ceramic floor tiles that present photo images of the outdoors.

▲ The Harvest table is from Barnwood Originals, which disassembles abandoned barns and reuses the historical wood.

▶ Rough-hewn stone and intentional aging are elements of a reproduction eighteenth-century Mexican aqua vera from The Elegant Earth.

▶ The raw properties of concrete are put to good use in table tops made from an ecologically designed, lightweight concrete material known as Syndecrete.

Photograph: Amedeo

▶ Ancient designs from Crete inspire the oil jar and beehive jar, while an 1850 piece is the model for the battle urn, all of which are made of lightweight fiberglass by Capital Garden Products.

▲ Il Piata paving stones from Ann Sacks Tile & Stone feature mottled design and color in frostproof material.

▶ Carmel seating recalls the smooth touch of weathered driftwood but is made of sand-cast aluminum in a design by John Caldwell for The Veneman Collection.

◄ Old Hickory's log-inspired Grove Park chair and ottoman combine with the Cricket table for a rich cabin look.

▲ Kim Hansen creates custom tile-and-stone tables for Casual Comforts in a variety of shapes, sizes, and colors.

Photograph: Mark Woods

◄ Resembling rough-hewn stone, the Alpine trough is made of cast, reconstituted limestone, and may be used on matching supports by Haddonstone or placed directly on the ground.

Mediterranean/Island

Hot weather and clear, blue water evoke days of island pleasure. Rich colors and textures recall Mediterranean vacations (or dreams).

▲ Created in Australia, the Down Under hanging pot from Kinsman Company is hand-crafted of natural terra cotta in the United States.

▲ Giati's Alisèo teak chair was designed by Mark Singer for a five-star Hawaiian hotel expressly for use on the lanais and features adjustable elements that make it appropriate for dining as well.

▲ Dez Ryan's Island Denizen hurricane lamp is handmade by the artist/designer and includes a blown glass globe and bright glass beads dangling from a leafy collar.

▶ Xavier Llongueras makes this large, sunburst-patterned coffee table from hand-cut pieces of Byzantine glass inlay resting on a base of brushed steel for Catalonia Collections.

◄ Waves undulate in the back of Provence dining chairs in cast aluminum, designed by John Caldwell for Tropitone.

► Recalling ancient mosaics and cracked tiles, Eco, offered by Ann Sacks Tile & Stone, is created from today's frost-proof material.

◄ Torquay porcelain serving pieces from Mottahedeh are decorated with images of sea life.

► Hand-crafted by Ann Morhauser for Annieglass, the Shell series evokes natural sea forms and is made from sandblasted glass reminiscent of found beach glass; gold edges add formality.

Photograph: R. J. Muna

◀ Recalling rattan furnishings, Jardin tables, cushion chairs, and chaise lounges by Brown Jordan are made from resin weaving material over aluminum frames.

▼ Terra-cotta pavers are brought up to date by Fiberstars, which uses fiber optic technology to incorporate lighting in its FiberScape paver system.

▲ Bamboo style is reinterpreted in cast aluminum stalks and leaves in a line of seating and tables designed by John Caldwell for The Veneman Collection.

WHIMSY

Outdoor living can't be taken too seriously, and these clever, lighthearted chairs, accessories, and tiles make adding joy and fun to your day easier.

▶ Majestic's Tulip Torches designed by David Tisdale stand pretty in their pots on tables and may also be accompanied by tulip string lights overhead.

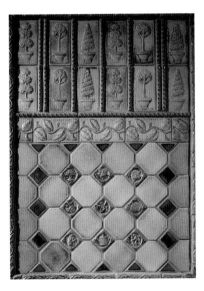

▲ Topiary Series tiles from Ann Sacks Tile & Stone complement any garden setting with its green hues and charming illustrations of trees, birds, gardeners, and tools.

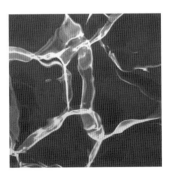

◀ Ironic in the extreme, Imagine Tile's Water design creates a pool-like illusion in glazed ceramic tile using up-to-date graphic technology.

▶ Richard Schultz evokes carved-and-shaped shrubbery in his Topiary designs in bent, stamped, and folded sheet aluminum available in clear or green finishes.

▼ Ann Morhauser of Annieglass designs Splash expressly for outdoor entertaining in fun fish shapes for bowls, platters, and plates.

Photograph: Diane Ritch

▲ Inherently playful, this chess table is made from hand-cut marble by Xavier Llongueras for Catalonia Collections.

▲ Fluid shapes in polished aluminum give an almost animated feeling to the Toledo Collection of tables and chairs designed by Jorge Pensi for Knoll.

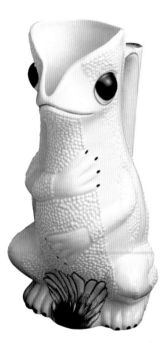

▲ Include an outdoor froggy friend on your table with this porcelain pitcher from Mottahedeh.

◄ Tiles are imbedded with recycled elements—such as twigs, nails, and glass chips—and made from Syndecrete, a lightweight concrete material developed by David Hertz, AIA.

Photograph: Tom Bonner

GEOMETRIC

Contemporary geometric furniture embraces many forms and materials, from cast aluminum to traditional teak. Sleek, clean lines blend well with outdoor spaces that are kept simple and spare.

▶ Mesa from Brown Jordan exhibits sophisticated styling in teak chairs and tables that are available in rectangular and circular shapes; tables come with a slate inset.

▼ These pre-cast planters embody pure forms. David Hertz, AIA, designed them and made them from Syndecrete, the lightweight concrete material he developed.

Photograph: Amedeo

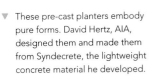

▲ Aptare's first outdoor line, the Laguna Collection designed by Lawrence O'Toole, includes deep-seating sofa, arm chair, and low table made of plantation-grown solid teak.

▶ Crisp, contemporary design and white finish of the Perception line by Tropitone complement Modern homes.

▲ Orlando Diaz-Azcuy uses a trellis motif—intersecting solid teak members framed by circular and rectangular backs—in the Portico Collection of indoor/outdoor furniture for McGuire.

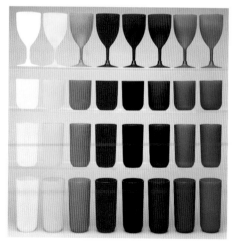

▲ Plastic Tabletop drinkware for the outdoors is designed in simple shapes by David Tisdale and manufactured by Majestic.

▲ Concentric circles shape the Adams top for the wrought-aluminum Hepplewhite side and coffee tables by McKinnon and Harris.

◀ Ilan Dei's cast aluminum Airfoil vase takes its dynamic shape from ship masts and is available in brushed, polished, and colored aluminum finishes.

▼ Teak furniture with cane inserts defines Giati's Azia line of tables and seating, which has stylistic echoes of both Asian and European design.

▲ Cool elegance and bright colors are hallmarks of Annieglass, designed by Ann Morhauser, whose long boats and triangle plates are handmade from slumped glass.

Photograph: R. J. Muna

▶ Straight lines are softened by subtle curves in the Nantucket chaise made of solid teak by Kingsley-Bate.

► John Kelly explores frames and surfaces in the K2 Series, including a garden settee made from slats of white oak.

▼ Mixtures of transparent and opaque glasses are combined in each of the small Dolce tiles from Ann Sacks Tile & Stone.

▲ A beautifully arced arabesque outlines the award-winning 1966 Collection by Richard Schultz in vinyl mesh on cast and extruded aluminum frames.

► Slatted apron detailing and curved benches are hallmarks of the mahogany Weatherend dining set, which uses full mortise-and-tenon joinery reinforced with marine-grade epoxy.

▲ The Drayton teak bench from Chelsea Ex-Centrics, constructed with traditional mortise-and-tenon joints and teak dowels, adds practicality with optional, detachable side tables.

▲ Hand-crafted in England from solid, all-weather teak, the London design dates back to the early 1920s, when it was first offered by Barlow Tyrie.

▶ High verticality is featured in Summit Furniture's Sources dining chairs, which complement the First Cabin dining table, all designed by Kipp Stewart.

DIRECTORY

DESIGN PROFESSIONALS

Joe Addo
Joe Addo Studio
9312 Civic Center Drive
Beverly Hills, CA 90210
310.274.4333

Michael and Hilary Anderson
Clacton & Frinton
107 South Robertson Boulevard
Los Angeles, CA 90048
310.275.1967

Hideaki Ariizumi
Gynis M. Berry
Studio A/B
111 Fourth Avenue
Number 2M
New York, NY 10003
212.677.7898

David E. Austin, AIA
Dana Marcu
Austin Patterson
    Associates Architects
376 Pequot Avenue
Post Office Box 61
Southport, CT 06490
203.255.4031

Barbara Barry
Barbara Barry Incorporated
9526 Pico Boulevard
Los Angeles, CA 90035
310.275.9977

Hagy Belzberg
Belzberg Architects
9615 Brighton Way
Suite 320
Beverly Hills, CA 90210
310.271.3087

James Blakeley, III, ASID
Blakeley-Bazeley, Ltd.
Post Office Box 5173
Beverly Hills, CA 90210
213.653.3548

Peter Q. Bohlin, FAIA
Bernard J. Cywinski, FAIA
Jon C. Jackson, AIA
Bohlin Cywinski Jackson
125 South Ninth Street
Philadelphia, PA 19107
215.592.0600

Stanley Boles
Kevin Johnson
John O'Toole
BOORA Architects, Inc.
720 Southwest Washington
Portland, OR 97205
503.226.1575

Pamela Burton
Burton & Company Landscape
    Architecture
2324 Michigan Avenue
Santa Monica, CA 90404
310.828.6373

Aviva Bornovski Carmy
Holly Bieniewski, AIA
Carmy Design Group
10793 Lindbrook Drive
Los Angeles, CA 90024
310.446.9556

Victoria Casasco
Victoria Casasco Studio
320D Sunset Avenue
Venice, CA 90291
310.399.1206

Richard Corsini
Richard Corsini Architect
2841 Avenel Street
Los Angeles, CA 90039
213.662.0752

Ilan Dei
1227 Abbot Kinney Boulevard
Venice, CA 90291
310.450.0999

Mayita Dinos
310.838.5959

Tony Duquette
1354 Dawnridge Drive
Beverly Hills, CA 90202
310.271.3574

Steven Ehrlich, FAIA
Steven Ehrlich Architects
2210 Colorado Avenue
Santa Monica, CA 90404
310.828.6700

John Erickson, AIA
Erickson Designs
24443 Zermatt Lane
Valencia, CA 91355

James Estes
James Estes and Company
    Architects
79 Thames Street
Newport, RI 02840
401.846.3336

Bernardo Fort-Brescia, FAIA
Laurinda Hope Spear, FAIA
Arquitectonica
550 Brickell Avenue
Suite 200
Miami, FL 33131
305.372.1812

Susan Jay Freeman, ASID
Susan Jay Design
9009 Beverly Boulevard
Los Angeles, CA 90048
310.858.1181

Ron Goldman, FAIA
Bob Firth, AIA
Clelio Boccato, AIA
Goldman Firth Boccato
    Architects
24955 Pacific Coast Highway
Suite A202
Malibu, CA 90265
310.456.1831

Alexander Gorlin
Alexander Gorlin Architect
137 Varick Street
New York, NY 10013
212.229.1199

David Lawrence Gray, FAIA
David Lawrence Gray
    Architects, AIA
1546 Seventh Street
Suite 101
Santa Monica, CA 90401
310.394.5707

David Hacin
Hacin & Associates Architects
46 Waltham Street
Suite 404
Boston, MA 02118
617.426.0077

David Hertz, AIA
Syndesis
2908 Colorado Avenue
Santa Monica, CA 90404
310.829.9932

Charlie Hess
C. Hess Design
516 North Mansfield
Los Angeles, CA 90036
213.930.1706

Aleks Istanbullu
Aleks Istanbullu John Kaliski
    Architecture and City Design
1659 Eleventh Street
Suite 200
Santa Monica, CA 90404
310.450.8246

Albert Janz, IIDA
Sherry Stein
Henry Johnstone & Company
95 San Miguel Road
Pasadena, CA 91105
626.395.9528

Noel Jeffrey
Noel Jeffrey Inc. Interior Design
215 East 58th Street
New York, NY 10022
212.935.7775

Sarah Boyer Jenkins, FASID
Edward Wesely
Sarah Boyer Jenkins and
    Associates, Inc.
8520 Connecticut Avenue
Suite 101
Chevy Chase, MD 20815
301.951.3880

Debbie Jones
310.476.1824

Chip Kalleen, IIDA
Old Hickory Furniture Co., Inc.
403 South Noble Street
Shelbyville, IN 46176
800.232.2275

Annie Kelly
2074 Watsonia Terrace
Hollywood, CA 90068
213.874.4278

Christine Kendall-Jent, ASID, IIDA
Santa Barbara Interiors
450 Paseo Del Descanso
Santa Barbara, CA 93105
805.569.1937

Mark D. Kirkhart, AIA
William S. Wolf
DesignARC, Inc.
One North Salsipuedes Street
Suite 210
Santa Barbara, CA 93103
805.963.4401

Sandy Koepke
Sandy Koepke Interior Design
1517 North Beverly Drive
Beverly Hills, CA 90210
310.273.1960

James Kwan
Kwan Design
409 North Lucerne Boulevard
Los Angeles, CA 90004
213.464.1032

David Lake
Ted Flato
Lake & Flato Inc.
311 Third Street
Suite 200
San Antonio, TX 78205
210.227.3335

Bill Lane
Bill Lane & Associates, Inc.
926 North Orlando Avenue
Los Angeles, CA 90069
310.657.7890

Ricardo Legorreta
Legorreta Arquitectos
Sierra Nevada No. 460
Lomas de Chapultepec, Mexico, DF
525.520.0745

Donn Logan
ELS/Elbasani & Logan
    Architects
2030 Addison Street
Berkeley, CA 94704
510.549.2929

Janet Lohman
Janet Lohman Interior Design
1021 South Fairfax
Los Angeles, CA 90019
213.933.3359

Mark Mack
Mack Architects
2343 Eastern Court
Venice, CA 90291
310.822.0094

Lise Claiborne Matthews, AIA, ASID
1510 Abbot Kinney Boulevard
Venice, CA 90291
310.399.7108

Roy McMakin
1422 34th Avenue
Seattle, WA 98122
206.323.0198

Lee F. Mindel, AIA
Shelton, Mindel & Associates
216 West 18th Street
New York, NY 10011
212.243.3939

Brian Alfred Murphy
Julie Hart
BAM Construction/Design Inc.
150 West Channel Road
Santa Monica, CA 90402
310.459.0955

Susan Narduli, AIA
Narduli/Grinstein Architects
2304 Zeno Place
Venice, CA 90291
310.827.9697

David R. Olson, AIA
David R. Olson Architects
6 Morgan
Suite 100
Irvine, CA 92618
714.587.3041

John O'Neill
James Palmer
John O'Neill Architectural Design
508 Mystic Way
Laguna Beach, CA 92651
714.497.6170

Gary Orr
Orr Design Office
2600 San Jose Way
Sacramento, CA 95817
916.452.3642

Polly Osborne, AIA
Osborne Architects
1833 Stanford Street
Santa Monica, CA 90404
310.828.2212

McKee Patterson, AIA
Austin Patterson Associates Architects
376 Pequot Avenue
Post Office Box 61
Southport, CT 06490
203.255.4031

Michael Palladino
Richard Meier + Partners Architects
1001 Gayley Avenue
Los Angeles, CA 90024
310.208.6464

Rob Pressman, ASLA
TGP, Inc.
6345 Balboa Boulevard
Suite 125
Encino, CA 91316
818.345.3602

Gwynne Pugh
Larry Scarpa
Pugh + Scarpa Architecture and
    Engineering
Bergamot Station
2525 Michigan Avenue
Building F1
Santa Monica, CA 90404
310.828.0226

Joseph Ruggiero
Joseph Ruggiero & Associates
4512 Louise Avenue
Encino, CA 91316
818.783.9257

Daniel Sachs
Snook
10 Greene Street
New York, NY 10013
212.343.2420

Martha Schwartz
Martha Schwartz, Inc.
147 Sherman Street
Suite 200
Cambridge, MA 02140
617.661.8141

Josh Schweitzer
Schweitzer BIM Inc.
5541 West Washington Boulevard
Los Angeles, CA 90016
213.936.6163

Russell Shubin, AIA
Robin Donaldson, AIA
Shubin + Donaldson Architects
629 State Street
Suite 242
Santa Barbara, CA 93101
805.966.2802

Kathleen Spiegelman
K. Spiegelman Interiors
623 North Almont
West Hollywood, CA 90069
310.273.2255

John Staff, AIA
J. Staff Architect
2148-C Federal Avenue
Los Angeles, CA 90025
310.477.9972

Òdom and Kate Stamps
Stamps & Stamps
318 Fairview Avenue
South Pasadena, CA 91030
818.441.5600

Timothy Morgan Steele
805.965.3888

Rob Steiner
Griffith & Steiner
717 California Avenue
Venice, CA 90291
310.450.0125

Stephen Suzman
Suzman Design Associates
233 Douglass Street
San Francisco, CA 94114
415.252.0111

Brian Tichenor
Raun Thorp
Tichenor & Thorp Architects
8730 Wilshire Boulevard
Penthouse
Los Angeles, CA 90211
310.358.8444

Jeffrey Michael Tohl, AIA
The Architecture Studio
8522 West Third Street
Los Angeles, CA 90048
310.652.7890

Sallie Trout
Trout Studios
5880 Blackwelder
Culver City, CA 90232
310.202.8868

Anne Troutman
Troutman & Associates
1721 Pier Avenue
Santa Monica, CA 90405
310.452.0410

William Turnbull, Jr.
Eric Haesloop
Turnbull Griffin & Haesloop Architects
Pier 1fi, The Embarcadero
San Francisco, CA 94111
415.986.3642

Raquel Vert
Raquel Vert Design
18039 Karen Drive
Encino, CA 91316
818.708.1177

Diego Villaseñor
Diego Villaseñor
    Arquitecto y Asociados
Tiburero Montiel 96
San Miguel
Chapultepec D.F.
11850, Mexico
52.5.272.98.44

Shepard Vineburg
Shepard Vineburg Design
232 Fifth Place
Manhattan Beach, CA 90266
310.318.6810

Mark Warwick
Kim Hoffman
The System Design
9828 Charleville Boulevard
Beverly Hills, CA 90212
310.556.7711

Vicente Wolf
Vicente Wolf Associates, Inc.
333 West 39th Street
New York, NY 10018
212.465.0590

Marcy Li Wong, AIA
Marcy Li Wong Architect
2251 Fifth Street
Berkeley, CA 94710
510.843.0916

PHOTOGRAPHERS

Ed Addeo
214 West 29th Street
New York, NY 10001
212.736.0897

Michael Arden
Arden Photography
14568 Greenleaf Street
Sherman Oaks, CA 91403
310.274.2064

Farshid Assassi
3321 Calle Rosales
Santa Barbara, CA 93105
805.682.2158

Karl A. Backus
Bohlin Cywinski Jackson
307 Fourth Avenue
Suite 1300
Pittsburgh, PA 15222
412.765.3890

Gordon Beall
4507 Sangsmore
Bethesda, MD 20816
301.229.0076

Laurie Black
172 Upper Lakeview Road
White Salmon, WA 98672
509.493.8670

Tom Bonner
1201 Abbot Kinney Boulevard
Venice, CA 90291
310.396.7125

Steven Brooke
79-10 Southwest 54th Court
Miami, FL 33143
305.667.8075

Chuck Choi
Chuck Choi Architectural
    Photography
204 Berkeley Place
Brooklyn, NY 11217
718.638.5825

Dan Cornish
Cornish Productions
38 Evergreen Road
New Canaan, CT 06840
203.972.3714

Christopher Covey
1780 Vista Del Mar Drive
Ventura, CA 93001
805.648.3067

Grey Crawford
2924 Park Center Drive
Los Angeles, CA 90068
310.558.1100

Charley Daniels
905 North Cole Avenue
Los Angeles, CA 90028
213.461.8659

Mimi Drop
157 North Sycamore
Los Angeles, CA 90036
213.857.0668

John Reed Forsman
420 North Fifth Street
Number 1088
Minneapolis, MN 55401
612.339.3999

Dan Francis
Mardan Photography
Post Office Box 20574
Indianapolis, IN 46220
317.251.8373

Sally Gall
47 Vestry Street
Number 2N
New York, NY 10013
212.334.4485

Fred George
737 Canal Street
Stamford, CT 06902
203.348.7454

Jay Graham
Six Bridge Avenue
Number 8
San Anselmo, CA 94960
415.459.3839

Michael Grecco
1701 Pier Avenue
Santa Monica, CA 90405
310.452.4461

Steven A. Gunther
Steven A. Gunther,
    Photography
22050 Ybarra Road
Woodland Hills, CA 91364
818.888.1029

Mick Hales
Greenworld Pictures Inc.
North Richardsville Road
RD 2
Carmel, NY 10512
800.370.8661

Jerry Harpur
44 Roxwell Road
Chelmsford, Essex
CM12NB England

Tim Harvey
739 Allston Way
Berkeley, CA 94710
510.849.9494

Douglas Hill
Douglas Hill Photography, Inc.
2324 Moreno Drive
Los Angeles, CA 90039
213.660.0681

Patrick House
Post Office Box 3759
South Pasadena, CA 91031
818.355.0183

Warren Jagger
Warren Jagger Photography, Inc.
150 Chestnut Street
Providence, RI 02903
401.351.7366

Lourdes Jansana
Gran Via 522
Barcelona, Spain 08011
317.2107

Len Jenshel
Len Jenshel Photography
309 West 93rd Street
Suite 4A
New York, NY 10025
212.316.7809

Lourdes Legorreta
Legorreta Arquitectos
Sierra Nevada No. 460
Lomas de Chapultepec
Mexico, DF
525.520.0745

David Livingston
1036 Erica Road
Mill Valley, CA 94941
415.383.0898

Mark Lohman
Mark Lohman Photography
1021 South Fairfax
Los Angeles, CA 90019
213.933.3359

Michael Lyon
P.O. Box 140339
Dallas, TX 75214
214.342.3064

Rick Mandelkorn
Richard Mandelkorn
    Photography
65 Beaver Pond Road
Lincoln, MA 01773
617.259.3310

Allan Mandell
1436 South East Ogden Street
Portland, OR 97202
503.236.3685

Joseph W. Molitor
c/o Angela Giral
Avery Library
Columbia University
1172 Amsterdam Avenue
MC 0301
New York, NY 10027

Michael Moran
245 Mulberry Street
Number 14
New York, NY 10012
212.226.2596

John Murdock
Murdock Coolidge
    Photography
412 West 25th Street
Number 6F
New York, NY 10001
212.245.4001

Mary E. Nichols
232 South Arden Boulevard
Los Angeles, CA 90004
213.871.0770

Dircum Over
4244 Via Marina
Box 320
Marina del Rey, CA 90292
310.821.3859

Peter Paige
Peter Paige Photography
269 Parkside Road
Harrington Park, NJ 07640
201.767.3160

Erhard Pfeiffer
Erhard Pfeiffer Photographer
946 South Ogden Drive
Los Angeles, CA 90036
213.931.3079

Anthony Pinto
4117 Division Street
Los Angeles, CA 90065
213.344.9514

Undine Pröhl
1930 Ocean Avenue
Number 302
Santa Monica, CA 90405
310.399.5031

Marvin Rand
1310 Abbot Kinney
Venice, CA 90291
310.396.3441

Derek Rath
4044 Moore Street
Los Angeles, CA 90066
310.305.1342

J. Scott Smith
J. Scott Smith Photography
711-1/2 Pier Avenue
Santa Monica, CA 90405
310.392.1300

Eric Staudenmaier
2920 Zane Grey Terrace
Altadena, CA 91001
818.296.0266

Fred Stocker
213.827.6289

Tim Street-Porter
2074 Watsonia Terrace
Hollywood, CA 90068
213.874.4278

Peter Vitale
Post Office Box 10126
Santa Fe, NM 87504
505.988.2558

David Wakely
544 Vermont St.
San Francisco, CA 94107
415.861.7503

Paul Warchol
Paul Warchol Photography, Inc.
133 Mulberry Street
Room 6
New York, NY 10013
212.431.3461

Alan Weintraub
1832-A Mason Street
San Francisco, CA 94133
415.553.8191

Charles S. White
154 North Mansfield
Los Angeles, CA 90036
213.937.3117

Product Sources

Annieglass
310 Harvest Drive
Watsonville, CA 95076
800.347.6133

Aptare
691 Saint Ann's Drive
Laguna Beach, CA 92651
714.497.6279

Archiped Classics
315 Cole Street
Dallas, TX 75207
214.748.7437

Barlow Tyrie
1263 Glen Avenue, Suite 230
Moorestown, NJ 08057
609.273.7878

Barnwood Originals
Box 906
Cochrane, Alberta
Canada, T0L 0W0
403.932.2470

Brown Jordan
9860 Gidley Street
El Monte, CA 91731
818.443.8971

Capital Garden Products
Schieren Associates, Ltd.
Post Office Box 400
Pottervielle, NJ 07979
800.524.1270

Casual Comforts
10025 Southeast Cindy Lane
Boring, OR 97009
503.663.6401

Catalonia Collections
1503 Cahuenga Boulevard
Los Angeles, CA 90028
213.469.5266

Chelsea Ex-Centrics
297 Kansas Street, Suite B
San Francisco, CA 94103
415.863.4868

Ilan Dei
1227 Abbot Kinney Boulevard
Venice, CA 90291
310.450.0999

The Elegant Earth
1301 First Avenue North
Birmingham, AL 35203
800.242.7758

Fiberstars, Inc.
2883 Bayview Drive
Fremont, CA 94538
510.490.0719

Frontier Barnwood
3205 Erie Street
Laramie, WY 82070
307.742.5248

Giati Designs, Inc.
614 Santa Barbara Street
Santa Barbara, CA 93101
805.965.6535

Haddonstone (USA) Ltd.
5362 Industrial Drive
Huntington Beach, CA 92649
714.894.3500

Imagine Tile
10 Exchange Place
Suite 2010
Jersey City, NJ 07302
800.680.8453

John Kelly Furniture Design
144 Cambers Street
New York, NY 10007
212.385.1885

Kingsley-Bate
5587-B Guinea Road
Fairfax, VA 22032
703.978.7200

Kinsman Company, Inc.
River Road
Point Pleasant, PA 18950
800.733.4146

Knoll, Inc.
1235 Water Street
East Greenville, PA 18041
800.445.5045

Lloyd/Flanders Industries
3010 Tenth Street
Menominee, MI 49858
800.526.9894

Majestic
80 Cherry Street
Bridgeport, CT 06605
203.367.7900

McGuire
1201 Bryant Street
San Francisco, CA 94103
415.626.1414

McKinnon and Harris Inc.
Post Office Box 4885
Richmond, VA 23220
804.358.2385

Mottahedeh
225 Fifth Avenue
New York, NY 10010
212.685.3050

Old Hickory Furniture Co., Inc.
403 South Noble Street
Shelbyville, IN 46176
800.232.2275

Reed Bros.
Turner Station
Sebastopol, CA 95472
707.795.6261

Richardson Allen
Post Office Box 236
Saco, ME 04072
207.284.8402

Dez Ryan Studio
156 Chambers Street
Third Floor
New York, NY 10007
212.693.0263

Annie Sabroux Studio
2001 Main Street
Santa Monica, CA 90405
310.399.7037

Ann Sacks Tile & Stone, Inc.
8120 Northeast 33rd Drive
Portland, OR 97211
800.278.8453

Richard Schultz
806 Gravel Pike
P.O. Box 96
Palm, PA 18070
215.679.2222

Summit Furniture, Inc.
5 Harris Court
Monterey, CA 93940
408.375.7811

Syndecrete
2908 Colorado Avenue
Santa Monica, CA 90404
310.829.9932

Terra Furniture, Inc.
17855 Arenth Avenue
City of Industry, CA 91748
818.912.8523

Tropitone Furniture
5 Marconi
Irvine, CA 92618
714.951.2010

The Veneman Collection
6392 Industry Way
Westminster, CA 92683
714.894.0202

Weatherend Estate Furniture
6 Gordon Drive
Rockland, ME 04841
207.596.6483

Wickets Garden Style
Post Office Box 1225
Middleburg, VA 20118
800.585.1225

Windsor Designs
475 Grant Avenue
Phoenixville, PA 19460
610.935.7777

INDEX